*A Better
Man, Woman
& Child*

Sylvia Durant

A Better
Man, Woman
& Child

*A Better
Man, Woman
& Child*

Sylvia Durant

*Publisher
Pocket Perks Etc.
Novi, Michigan*

*A Better
Man, Woman
& Child*

Copyrights 2004
Sylvia Durant
All Rights Reserved

ISBN
0-9641133-9-2

Dedication

I dedicate this book to my grandmother, Gertrude Durant the lady that taught me Love never fails, my son, Remerro Trosky Williams who always shares his great gift of wisdom with me and to my precious aunt, Ione Williams my mother of love that is always present for me.

Author's Notes

This book was written to be a blessings to every one that feast their eyes upon these special words. May they be touched by love, inspired by wisdom, and surrounded by Joy.

Contents

Book 1

*A Better Man
Noble Authority*

Book 11

*A Better Woman
Appreciated Results*

Book 111

*A Better Child
Delicate Balance*

The Parents Edition

†

A Better Man

Noble Authority

Book 1

†

A Better Man

Almighty God, our heavenly father made man first, woman second, and then came the little child.

Walk in the light of your life, and your purpose will come forth and mankind will know exactly who you are.

†

A Better Man

*In order to be like yourself,
you have to know who you are.*

*Men, the best time to be happy
is while you are living.*

†

A Better Man

A man's good attitude will make it easy for people to help him, and his bad attitude will slam doors and cut off pathways.

A man's smile can change the environment and the circumstance of any important matter.

†

A Better Man

A sudden act without thought, can cause a sudden mistake with many regrets.

The tongue is a little member of your body, that speaks big decisions in your life.

†

A Better Man

A woman on a man's arm is a sight,
a woman in a man's heart is beautiful.

Handsome clothes won't make the man but,
they sure will make him look good.

Durant / A Better Man, Woman & Child

✝

A Better Man

The man that gives from his heart pleases God, the man that gives from his hand pleases man.

The undressed truth is so direct and the edges can cut so very deep but, the revelation is yours.

†

A Better Man

*Treat your woman like a rose and
she will bloom for you.*

*Beyond yourself are those who love you,
discover their love by seeking it.*

†

A Better Man

The man that works to make today better, knows that the end can be as far away as right now.

The direction of a man's time is so precious, it will help determine his life.

†

A Better Man

The appearance of a man is easy to judge,
the truth about a man is insight.

A man with noble authority can
commission unquestionable obedience,
due to his great integrity.

†

A Better Man

String your thoughts with countless pearls
and your days will be precious.

String your thoughts with useless pebbles
and your days will be rocky.

†

A Better Man

No man will ever see another man laugh,
cry, or breathe in another language.

Some men know a lot about what's
not important, and not enough about
what is important.

†

A Better Man

In this daring and delicate world we live in we need to spend more time loving and less time lashing.

Exceeding your service to others reflects your grace and inspires great moments of extendible love.

†

A Better Man

Watch who and what you are attracted too, it can challenge your mind, affect your body and stir up your spirit.

Always follow your heart, for it keeps in touch with all truth, and delivers you from falsity.

†

A Better Man

An effective state of affairs must have an appropriate time to be received.

Honored time and cherished moments bring great and lasting pleasure.

†

A Better Man

A million dollars starts with the first penny,
what happens after that is up to you.

Money has a notorious reputation for being
loved, being spent and being stolen.

†

A Better Man

A full spectrum of human emotions can be felt in just a few moments.

Time spent with a person gives you Closeness, time spent away from a person give you space.

†

A Better Man

We are responsible for what we don't know,
and obliged to what we do know.

A man can be sharp in intellect and
dull in integrity, great in business
and lacking at home.

✝

A Better Man

The truth is timeless and
will never change it's ways.

True words touched by love are
anointed and blessed with wisdom.

†

A Better Woman

Appreciated Results

Book 11

†

A Better Woman

She, who uses the divine power that Almighty God has given her, in a honorable way, will get blessed results.

The influence that women have on
this world will never be silenced,
for it is embedded in the seed of man.

†

A Better Woman

A woman's made up mind and determination can get her anywhere she really wants to go, with no advantages left out.

A woman has the prerogative to change her mind for the good and that's intentional thinking.

†

A Better Woman

Keep a ready smile that comes from your heart,
someone may need it other than yourself.

Don't let your joy be stolen by the thief
of sadness, a women's smile is a delight.

†

A Better Woman

A woman with many shoes,
may have hurting feet.

A woman with a grateful heart,
will have many blessings.

†

A Better Woman

Why do we wonder why things are not done,
when we don't do them.

The only way to proceed successfully is to
move in a forward direction carefully.

†

A Better Woman

The taste of love is bitter sweet,
the truth of love is unconditional.

The touch of love reflects your heart,
the rejection of love reflects your mind.

†

A Better Woman

Trouble never comes at a convenient time,
but time is always convenient for trouble.

Don't speak before you think, speak after
you think and your words will be in order.

✝

A Better Woman

A friend is like a sweet song, they hit
high notes and low tones but
the melody tarries on.

True friendship is a kinship that will
get better with age and last with love.

†

A Better Woman

God will send you the right husband, when you are ready to be the right wife.

❦

What makes a man rich is his love for the Lord, all other things will follow.

†

A Better Woman

The way a woman dresses may not be the way she wants to be seen.

❦

The way a woman is seen should not determine who she is.

†

A Better Woman

A woman with a man is noted,
a woman without a man is still a woman.

❦

A woman that expect a man to
be other than who he really is,
awaits disappointments.

†

A Better Woman

A woman that continually checks her thinking can develop her mind.

A woman that purposely captures her good thoughts can dismiss her bad thoughts.

†

A Better Woman

The greatest day to be alive is today.

Be thankful for your breath,
it maintains your
life.

†

A Better Woman

Appreciated results is what happens after the deed has taken place and the reflection is clear.

A woman that sustains excellence and unswerving integrity will interlock appreciation.

†

A Better Woman

A better woman must not let her excitement
overwhelm her better judgment.

Joy is so sweet it brings tears to your eyes,
laughter to your heart and
peace to your mind.

†

A Better Woman

Human failure has no respect for who you are,
it wants to stop who you are going to be.

※

Temperament and tenderness may collide
or enhance conspicuous traits.

†

A Better Woman

Being a mother is more than just
having a child it's nurturing,
mentoring and most of all loving.

A woman can become a mother without
giving birth, all it takes is love,
appreciation and dedication.

Durant / A Better Man, Woman & Child

†

A Better Woman

Your self image is one of the best friends you will ever have, you must be good to it.

Your true success has favor, peace of mind, integrity and revelation.

†

A Better Woman

Reaching wise decision and just conclusions characterizes deep understanding.

❦

The characteristics of a woman will distinctively mark her traits and highlight her attributes.

†

A Better Woman

Some things you will know when you see them, other things you won't recognize until after they are passed.

Just because something is free, doesn't make it good for you, it could be bad for you and good for someone else.

†

A Better Woman

Good laughter is so inspiring it promotes divine health.

Good laughter done in good taste is a joyful experience.

†

A Better Woman

Dare to be yourself, for there is no other woman on this earth like you.

Dancing in the light of your life, will elaborate your dreams and fulfill your purpose.

†

A Better Child

Delicate Balance

Book 111

The Parents Edition

†

A Better Child

Almighty God made your child to be someone different and to do something special.

A better child will be characterized by the distinctive qualities displayed by his parents.

†

A Better Child

Becoming a parent is the beginning of what you don't know about children.

Babies know their mother first, after birth they are introduced to their father.

†

A Better Child

Before a child is born he is already somebody.

❦

A better child is carefully molded not hammered.

†

A Better Child

There is always a space waiting
for the unborn child.

At birth babies know to cry, breathe,
and move their very being.

†

A Better Child

The original conception of a child maybe duplicated, but never originated.

The innocence of a child has great beauty and harmless intentions.

†

A Better Child

Parents are the blue print by which children go by, construct it well and the foundation will stand.

A delicate balance is so important to both the parents and children, for it keeps the weight of life even.

†

A Better Child

The things you did not understand as a child, you will know as a parent.

Parenting is an experience that will never end, it holds the delicacies of life.

†

A Better Child

Teach a child integrity and his
virtues will definitely show.

A child that accepts direct instructions
will bear sound corrections.

†

A Better Child

Your good manners will affect your child's daily behavior.

When you listen carefully to your child you will hear yourself.

A Better Child

Teaching a child right from wrong is not an option, it is a commitment.

The class room is more than just a field of study, it's a place of progress.

†

A Better Child

Where in this world is your child?
Maybe it's you that's missing.

Spending time with your child is
really getting to know yourself.

†

A Better Child

Teach a child to invest both in finances and integrity and the long term dividends will be more than rewarding.

Teaching a child financial responsibility, starts with the little money you put into his little hands.

†

A Better Child

A child's play is an exercise of a creative effort and a talent unknown.

A child's talent is a characteristic feature that is a natural endowment waiting to be enriched.

✝

A Better Child

The most important legacy we can leave
our children is love, wisdom and joy.

Love will never fail you, wisdom will
always direct you and joy comes
with peace of mind.

†

A Better Child

The children of this world are the
seeds of our land, let us nourish their roots,
with goodness, for they will till the next generation.

Almighty God purposely created our children
to fulfill their birth rights of love, wisdom,
and joy, so that their place in this
world will be acclaimed.

Durant / A Better Man, Woman & Child

†

Blessings

Thank you for choosing to read A Better Man, Woman & Child. This book was inspired by the word of God and written in the spirit of love. May we all breathe God's love, experience his joy and caress his word throughout our lives.

Sylvia Durant is a Creative Writing Consultant, Speaker and Author born in Washington, D.C. and resides in Novi, Michigan.

I, Sylvia Durant love you dearly.

"Happy Reading"

For special orders please call

248.305.7116
SDurant333@aol.com

"Thank You"